EVERY
CHILD
NEEDS
A LILY

Every Child Needs a Lily

People Helping People to Succeed

Lillie White-Evans

Illustrator: Jason Kelly Vallas

ISBN 978-1-0980-6625-3 (paperback)
ISBN 978-1-0980-6626-0 (digital)

Christian Faith Publishing, Inc.
832 Park Avenue
Meadville, PA 16335
www.christianfaithpublishing.com

Printed in the United States of America

CONTENTS

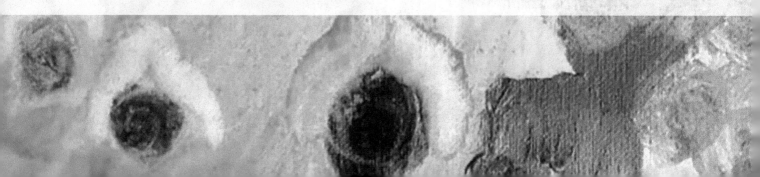

INTRODUCTION

Every Child Needs a Lily is a collaborative effort of a mentor and of her mentees to stress that every person needs at least one person to challenge and encourage them to become successful. The book is a spinoff of a business idea, Total Image Care Educational Consulting Company (TICECC) LLC, developed by the mentor in 2003 but was never up and operating due to illness.

The mentor is a retired classroom teacher and administrator with thirty plus years of experience who decided to utilize the following famous quotes:

"Bloom where you are planted" by St. Francis de Sales (1567-1622). The Bishop of Geneva is credited with the quote, "Bloom where you are planted." Several people have used this from a religious as well as a political standpoint to mean one should do their best in whatever situation or circumstance they find themselves. It doesn't mean they can't be transplanted elsewhere later and bloom in the new location, but to do your best and thrive right where you are. This idiom or quote has served as a guiding force to help the author work herself from many predicaments and find resolutions to problems.

"When you learn, teach." A quote by Maya Angelou, a twentieth century African-American poet and author, which was so in keeping with what the author believes that she felt compelled to do just that whenever the opportunity afforded itself.

She began meeting with two sisters and teaching them a wide range of life skills including self-esteem activities and biblical knowledge. Students were taught how to make some Southern dishes such as Cajun Okra, Gumbo, etc. They were also taught how to clean a house, how to shop for good grocery/produce, and proper etiquette such as writing "Thank You" notes. Most activities were held on Saturdays to avoid school constraints. Other activities included watching movies and going for lunch. Students helped the mentor to shop for appropriate gifts for baby showers, birthdays, etc. Every activity was a teaching /learning situation. The activities served purpose for the mentees but overall the mentor saw it as an extension of her goal to give back some of the extra care and concern shared with her by her teachers and administrators growing up as a student at Natchez Junior High School, in Natchez, LA.

The ultimate goal of this book is to challenge other educators and retired educators to commit to helping at least one child beyond school to become the best they can be. The answer to the growing numbers of social ills in our society cannot rest only with school administrators, teachers, and school personnel. Other community agencies must increase programs and activities for children and youth to eliminate the many social ills plaguing America. Statistics prove that it takes at least one person to encourage a child to succeed. If every retired educator and every teacher became a mentor to at least one child beyond the classroom, think how many children would become successful.

<u>Every Child Needs a Lily</u> is a statement made by Sherron Williams, one of the author's mentees who was thanking her for her service, after describing the horrors she was experiencing as a young, newly appointed attorney. (You will hear from her later.)

CHAPTER 1

ABOUT THE MENTOR

I always knew I was going to become a teacher. When I was about five years old, I exclaimed to my Uncle Jeffery, "I am going to be a teacher, Uncle Jeffery!" "Ha! Ha! Ha, Uncle knows because you've already got two pencils!" I did not learn until later that he was referring to my legs. I was a skinny child; however, I grew up and became that teacher.

I strongly believe that my experiences as a student growing up in Rural Louisiana as a sharecropper's daughter helped to fuel my desire even more. I attended Natchez Jr. High School from about third grade to eighth grade. The care and concern by the faculty and staff were absolutely above reproach. Those adults provided an "environment of excellency" and not only provided cognitive skills but life skills. I gained more respect and appreciation for the many activities teachers provided above and beyond their duties and responsibilities. They taught the **Whole Child** (physically, mentally, socially/emotionally, and spiritually) and they truly cared for the students. Nowhere was it written to teach proper use of eating utensils and etiquette; yet, I remember teachers doing just that before taking students to the cafeteria. Since most of the teachers themselves had come from environments like their students, they sincerely imparted their knowledge about life in general, as well as their subject matter.

The Black public school was truly the gateway to learning for students who grew up in the 1950s and 60s. Teachers had support from parents to teach and discipline students and prepare them for life. Schools became second homes for many of us.

My mother died when I entered fourth grade. My teacher went above and beyond her role as teacher to make me knowledgeable not only about school subjects, but about life after school. She often invited me to her home with her family or on trips with her family. I attended the same church as they did; therefore, she followed my education and provided opportunities for me to grow spiritually. Because she liked to win, I like to win (anything); she liked being the best at whatever she did; I don't half-do anything. She immersed herself in my life and personally took me to college (she and her family). Many thought they were my family.

There is a saying that children imitate their parents and leaders. They do what they do and not what they teach. Perhaps this is true, and I owe most of who I am to the great teachers and educators like Mr. Rudolph Leon Jr., Mrs. Rebecca Walker, Mr. David Nolley Jr., Mrs. Doris Beard, Mrs. Dorothy Moffett, Mrs. Moselle Lawson-Anderson, Mrs. Nudia Bell Bradley, Mrs. Thelma Thrash, Mr. Oscar Wright, and Mrs. Ethel Frazier.

This is a tribute to every Black teacher who worked in rural schools and gave of their time, money, and talents to teach the **Whole Child** and meet their needs as they saw them. As a child from such an environment who later became a classroom teacher, Language Arts coordinator, assistant principal, and school administrator in an Integrated Educational Environment, I can see that care and concern for the **Whole Child** was replaced with emphasis only on the physical and mental domains of learning. The social/emotional and spiritual domains of learning were missing because the white administrators saw no need for enhancing these skills since most white children were afforded these developments at home. Gone were the days of teaching manners and correcting any child who misspoke or misbehaved, taking a class outside to pick pecans during Health and Fitness, and allowing them to freely talk and socialize with the teachers or classmate (whoever came closest as we searched for pecans), no more reminders to dress your best for School Picture Day, and patriotic songs and spirituals were rarely sung and only on special programs.

Some children in this twentieth century education can go twelve years to a public school and never experience singing in a group as part of an audience. Many are required to stand for the national anthem but do not know the words to the song by second grade, which students in the 1950s and 60s were required to know. It is sad to see that cursive writing, music, arts, and dance have been removed from most elementary school curricula. These skills were once taught to aid in physical, mental, and social/emotional developments. I can remember being made to follow directions to such moves as "Swing your partner round and round" in dances like the Square Dance. The White schools discarded some albums along with the discarded used textbooks. Good teachers used these for teaching the following of directions as enhancement activities for English. Many students were afforded their first supervised social experience of dancing with the opposite sex.

Chapter 2

Being a Good Neighbor and Friend

I once thought being a good neighbor meant being kind to the people who lived closest to me; however, I now know a neighbor is anyone you encounter and get to know through some situation or circumstance. It seems that since God has chosen us and not we ourselves, we must trust Him to use us to His satisfaction. He pours through us to others what we receive when we are not even aware. We will never be able to measure spiritual success because we never know when our words, thoughts, actions, and deeds impact others or hundreds of other lives.

I often tell people who compliment me on my spirituality, "Honey, if you see anything good in me, it has to be Jesus because I know Lillie." The more I live, the more I know I can do nothing unless empowered by the Holy Spirit who represents the Kingdom of God. I have had some wonderful realizations of God's power and might, and I am aware of what I am representing. Apart from the grace of God, I can truly say: "But for the grace of God there go I. I am as bad as any criminal in possibility apart from God in me."

Good mentoring is simply sharing and helping people whenever you meet them. Mentoring takes on a life of its own when you purposely choose to pour into the lives of others, Always friendships are born. What you are taught as a child becomes an important part of your fiber. I was taught, both in school and at home, "Do unto others as you would have them do unto you and love your neighbor as yourself." They are indeed now a part of every fiber of my being.

JOYCE CARTER

When I think of Lillie, my mind goes to the lily plant that grows from a bulb. That bulb for us planted and grew years ago when our sons became friends in middle school. Our families blended into one happy family. My daughter became Lillie's daughter's big sister.

Lillie is a prayer warrior. She is always there to give a prayer for your healing and words of encouragement for any difficulty in your life.

Lillie, you are like the white lily, pure and lovely.

Thank you for the many years of caring and sharing!

Love and blessings,
Joyce Carter

COMMIE HOLMON

Everyone needs a Lillie…

There's a quote that simply says:
"Good friends are like stars—
You don't always see them, but
you know they're always there."

Everyone needs a Lillie in their life. Someone who is like those stars after forty plus years, Lillie has shown what a good friend is:

* Offers encouragement when things just seem to go wrong
* Knows how to express the brighter side of a dark situation
* Shares her faith
* Loves you for "you"

To my "star"—shine on

Your forever friend,
Commie

CHAPTER 3

PEOPLE ARE LOOKING AND LEARNING WHEN YOU ARE UNAWARE

In my many years of working to make sure that good teaching and learning in the classroom was a reality, I was focused more on my assigned role for the assigned room. As a teacher, I cared more about what I was supposed to be doing for my students than what the principal or visiting supervisor thought, and as a supervisor I always enjoyed the classes where the teachers seemed to have forgotten that I was present. I learned later that while I was observing the classrooms, both students and teachers were oftentimes observing me too.

We communicate different things to different people upon entering their environment. They bring to the visit a set of experiences and we have no control over their thoughts. They see what they see and we know what we know and what we want them to know, but unless those present communicate, we may never ever know.

I entered the work space of many teachers and students communicating by my presence what I was sometimes unaware; it was not until years later that I received both written and oral communication of many rewarding experiences. However, at the time, I was unaware that such was happening and I was playing such a role.

VANESSA WALKER

Ms. Lillie has been such a true and meaningful blessing in my life. As a young lady in Missionettes and Stars, I had the honor and privilege in Christ. She was faithful to love me and every girl under her faithful leadership each Wednesday night. I am forever grateful and thankful to her for teaching me how to pray out loud with confidence in a group. We would take prayer requests each time we would gather, hold hands, and take turns praying out loud in a standing circle for each and every request. Because of this activity, I am an adult who values coming together with other believers and bringing our requests before the Lord. I don't struggle with praying out loud because it felt so natural as a child. I don't believe this would be the case if we hadn't done this together so faithfully. Ms. Lillie has been a role model for me all of my life. She has shown me what it looks like to love faithfully while standing strong in who she is in the Lord. She is a pillar of truth in my life and I will always love her dearly and be very thankful that God put her in my life at an early age to help form my foundation in Christ. She was and is an example of how a confident and non-compromising woman of God lives her life and loves others. She is a rare jewel that blesses all she knows and loves. I love you always Ms. Lillie!

CHAPTER 4

LOVE YOUR NEIGHBOR AS YOURSELF

I think the commandment of Jesus **"to love your neighbor as yourself"** can best be illustrated by mothers of children and their playmates. When your child loves a playmate, as a mother, you develop a love also for your child's friend and often their mother. One can often tell a lot about the heart of a mother from being around her children.

When you find yourself as a mother praying as hard for your child's friend or playmate as your own, I believe this to be an example of loving your neighbor as yourself. Such was the case for me. My children's friends became like family, whom I treated as my own. Some of whom have remained lifelong friends and family.

KARI HARPER

My name is Kari Harper, formerly Kari Johnston. I met Ms. Evans in 1997–1998. My dad, Tom Johnston, married Georgia, and we (my dad, my sister Ashleigh, and I) moved into Georgia's townhome. Georgia's neighbor was Ms. Evans. Ms. Evans was instantly so nice and welcoming to us! She also let her faith shine so bright you couldn't help but "catch" it! Anytime I visited with her, she always was thankful to God or praising God for this or that.

After a little while my Dad and Georgia bought another home and sold the townhouse and we were no longer neighbors with Ms. Evans. I also got married. For some reason I decided to send Ms. Evans' Christmas cards each year, even though I did not see her or talk to her much anymore. It is as if God knew that I would need her words of wisdom, her comfort, and her prayers over the years as life would unfold and troubled times would come. And it did. And her Christmas cards would always be like a hug from someone who genuinely cared and wanted to comfort me.

I still have and read occasionally a prayer book that she sent me years ago—it has moved with me throughout Louisiana (North and South), Tennessee, and now Oklahoma! For some reason, for whatever reason Ms. Evans is someone that I think of when I am in need of good thoughts—although she and I don't know each other well! Over the years we have kept each other up on our lives through our Christmas cards and maybe Easter cards here and there. I find her words always comforting and encouraging and I find myself seeking them out and looking forward to them! Although I have not seen Ms. Evans in years, I still think of her often and admire her faith and I strive to be as faithful as she.

My relationship with Ms. Evans is an example of how a seemingly minor and fleeting relationship can have a lasting impact on someone's life. I wonder if she even knows just how much she crosses my mind and puts a smile on my heart? She was always so kind, so beautiful, so elegant…I imagine she is still that way and I bet her faith is immeasurable!

I am so very thankful that I had the opportunity to meet Ms. Evans and continue to benefit from her all these years.

If only the world could be so fortunate to meet a "Ms. Evans" of their own.

Sincerely,
Kari Harper

DJENIELE HOOTEN

Lillie Evans, known to me and so many others as Aunt Lillie, is the perfect example of what the Bible says about a Proverbs 31 woman.

As brilliant as she is beautiful, her loving heart is what always shines the most. Her heart for seeing God's will being done on this earth is what teaches so many to stay on their knees in talks with Him.

A little over fourteen years ago, Aunt Lillie and I began our journey that would grow into something very beautiful; only to have a literal life pin and a few detours put in there. Soon we would find our way back as the Lord would allow our paths to cross yet once again!

Being that my entire family were Pacific North Western transplants to the Deep South, we would soon find that it was going to take a little time getting use to our new world. Aunt Lillie was the perfect guide on our journey. She would teach us all about being the perfect Southern Belle, who would help us navigate through this new life with nothing more than pure grace!

We were new to this world…where we didn't know anyone. And no one knew us…but Lillie Evans; (Aunt Lillie) opened her arms, her heart, and her loving home to our entire family! She could be found embracing us for who we were, helping mold us into who we would need to be.

Chapter 5

The Classroom Is More Than Lessons, People, and Furniture

What is seen in a classroom is not nearly as interesting as the unseen. In a class of twenty-five to thirty students (which was the class size when I was a teacher), one question could invoke ten or more thoughts or memories. For example, finding the subject of a sentence about a dog could invite memories of a beautiful dog, a lost dog, a pet that died, etc.

It is the task of the teacher to prevent students from lingering on their thoughts. However, each student takes away much more than what is in that classroom due to previous experiences and knowledge about what is presented, or lack of previous experiences or knowledge. Try as they might, a teacher cannot control all thoughts, impressions, misconceptions, or beliefs in a given class period nor the entire school year or learning period. Therefore each student leaves a learning setting with some similar factual learning, but different impressions of the class itself as stated in the next case.

ANGELA L. DOUGLAS

My first encounter with Lillie Evans occurred about thirty years ago. Wow! That in itself says a lot. We met when I was a new teacher working for Caddo Parish Schools, assigned to Forest Hill Elementary. During this time, this was one of the schools that Ms. Evans supervised. I remember at our first meeting I was struck by her physical stature and mannerisms. Physically, she was a strikingly beautiful woman. Her clothing was tailored and fit well. She was the model of the adage "dress for success." Her professionalism was made known as soon as she began speaking. She spoke direct, no nonsense manner. One did not have to try to figure out what she was saying or attempt to read between the lines. As a new teacher, I was quite intimidated. Yet, it was just what I needed to help me in my growth as an educator.

Additionally, some years later, Ms. Evans was in charge of the Homeless Education program for the district and I was given the opportunity to work for her in providing a summer program for homeless children under the Stuart B. McKinney Act. For two summers, I worked with the homeless students under the leadership and guidance of Lillie Evans. She had a real passion for her work and for giving these students an educational experience that was both fun and academically enriching for the summer. Again, I grew a little more as I worked with these students who needed a little more love, patience, and understanding. My "Lillie" encounter did not end there.

Through those experiences and others, I got to know a different side of Ms. Evans. I must concur that everyone does need a "Lillie." Per the information I gleamed from the Internet, *"the oil of lilies actually has been found to have healing and softening properties."* Ms. Evans is filled with the oil of the Holy Spirit. During our thirty plus years of knowing one another, she has used that oil to advise, pray, listen, and share God's Word with my family and me. Her wisdom, knowledge of God's Word, and direct speech has helped heal various situations that we have shared with her.

At some point, and I cannot pinpoint the exact year, Ms. Evans became a mentor for my children and me. When I think about it, it has been an amazing experience. The mentorship and wise counsel began when my oldest daughter, Sherron Phae, began visiting Ms. Evans and doing little things around the house for her. Ms. Evans developed a mentor/ mentee relationship with her that lasted through her remaining high school years, undergraduate school, law school, and now marriage.

After Sherron went to college, my middle daughter, Jasmine, began going to Ms. Evans' home and doing little work for her. She worked, but did not realize that she too was in the midst of a developing mentor/mentee relationship. She learned to listen well and use the knowledge and wisdom that Ms. Evans would impart in order to become more successful. She, too, enjoyed a relationship that lasted through high school, undergraduate school, and continues today as she currently provides a sounding board with godly advice and prayers inspired by God's Holy Spirit as Jasmine navigates Medical School. You would think that working with two children from the same household would leave some weary. Not Ms. Evans.

Additionally, she has worked with my youngest daughter, Anastasia, in helping her navigate those extraordinarily curious middle school years. Anastasia really needed and benefited from having a "Lillie."

During that time Ms. Evans began working with her, I was a principal at an elementary school, working nonstop, including weekends. As a mother and educator, I kept up with her academic studies to make sure she was always excelling. However, I did not realize how much I did not have a handle on the numerous social problems and peculiar nuances that are associated with the middle school experience. Ms. Evans has a background in middle school and as far as I am concerned a PhD in children. She expertly assisted Anastasia with a myriad of middle school issues involving friendships, hurt feelings, attitudes (hers included), and appropriate responses to her teachers and parents. The impact she has had on her life will help guide her during the next phase of her school career and beyond.

As I look back, I am reminded, "*Hear counsel, and receive instruction, that thou mayest be wise in thy latter end. There are many devices in a man's heart; nevertheless the counsel of the Lord, that shall stand*" (Proverbs 19:20–21). The counsel that Ms. Evans has provided to my children and me has had a tremendous influence on our everyday lives. All of us can point to advice she has given that helped them get through some strenuous time whether academic tests, strained relationships, or illness. Her influence has also helped us in our pursuit to live a Godly life. Yes, everyone needs a "Lillie." We thank God for ours.

STEPHANIE COSME

1977 was the year that marked the beginning of my tour at Ridgewood Junior High School. That era often referred to as "the wonder years" where one who is fully happy and adjusted to the beat of elementary school is suddenly uprooted from their comfort zone and forced to somewhat reinvent themselves. I had been very involved in Summer Grove Elementary and was often out of class more than I was in class, busy about whatever my hands could find to do.

Often, I was called upon for a special project request from Mrs. Chocolate, our beloved principal. I had been forced to go to Walnut

Hill Junior High due to zoning regulations and had not done well there. My honor roll status had plummeted, and my mother had arranged for me to go to Ridgewood, the school I had originally wanted to attend. Being overweight was both a blessing and curse. It made me receptive to the underdog kids who did not fit in. I would always be nice to them and introduce them to my circle of friends, which was usually plentiful and quite diverse. The bad side was the bullying and abuse I was often subjected to by some of my peers. Again, I was not one of those kids that wanted to hurt myself, but I was often disheartened when people were unkind. I began at Ridgewood in the second report card period and my grades began to become normal again. I was working in the library and loved my art class. I was blessed with the most delightful English teacher. English was one of my favorite subjects. I did not mind diagraming sentences or spelling tests, having been in the spelling bee in fifth grade.

When I met Lillie Evans, it was obvious that she was not just there to babysit. She was very young and pretty with a certain calm and sweet spirit. She was beautiful on the inside and the outside. Lillie and I would often talk about my writing. She encouraged me to use my creative writing skills. She told me that I was a very good writer. I remember her introducing us to poetry and showing us that contrary to popular belief, poetry does not always have to rhyme. This opened a whole new genre of writing to me. I enjoyed one of the projects she had us do, which incorporated illustrations. Combining two of my favorite subjects was a definite plus. The more I got to know Lillie, I realized she was a very spiritual person. I would share with her stories about going to church and about my family. We talked about the Lord and related topics. She was a good listener. She had a soft spot for the misfit people in our class as well. I can remember how she dealt with a rowdy six pack of boys who would be disruptive. These boys were class clowns who were intelligent but liked to be mischievous. She did not let them get to her like some of the other teachers did. Their response was to send them to the office for discipline right off the bat. Not Lillie, she tried to get on their level and find ways to engage them in class. She took a girl under her wing who was experiencing anxiety and other issues which caused the kids to tease and bully her. The same girl lost her mother that year and Lillie was very patient and kind to her, helping her navigate the grief that had been thrust upon her already skewed life.

I always looked forward to coming to Lillie's class. I even hoped to have her again for the next year. That did not happen, but I would often see her and talk to her in the halls. Several years later I joined the choir at my church. I did a double take when low and behold there in the soprano section of the choir loft stood Lillie. I was so excited to see my sweet teacher. What a blast from the past! We attended church together and Lillie would often attend prayer group and what a prayer warrior she was. When she laid her hands on you, you could feel the presence of the Holy Spirit as she prayed specifically for your needs. Lillie served in many compassion ministries within the church. She was always there for those who needed free wise counsel and direction. I left that church some years ago. I had not seen Lillie since then. One day I was leaving the church I presently attend, and there was Lillie. She was seated on the back row, wearing a beautiful hat which enhanced her natural beauty. We embraced and marveled at the fact that our paths had once again crossed. Lillie and I have a special connection. I am so glad to have her back in my life. She still loves to mentor young people and has no problem going to life groups or other meetings where the attendees are much younger than she. I am honored that she has chosen me to help her in some of the things she has prayerfully considered starting at the church. Lillie continues to blossom, weaving her gifts of encouragement, discernment and prayer into the lives of those she encounters along the path.

CHAPTER 6

LESSONS FROM THE MENTEES

Each child is unique and I spend every chance I get to say something to that effect at every meeting. Some time is also spent helping them to get to know who made them unique and arranged for me to get to know them and love them…God. Each child is taught to pray among other different lessons and activities. Since I see students individually, lessons settings are designed specifically around what my assessments seemed they needed to learn or suggestions from their parents. Although the mentees are from the same family for the purpose of their writing, and received some of the same lessons and activities, they brought to the sessions varying experiences and as you will see took away different perspectives

SHERRON PHAE WILLIAMS

I met Ms. Lillie Evans when I was in high school. My mom introduced me to her, because Ms. Evans was my mom's mentor. I soon began visiting Ms. Evans on the weekends. During our visits, we had so much fun! We cooked, talked about everyday happenings, and discussed the Word of God. Some of my favorite memories are learning some of her recipes. She is such a good cook, and she made cooking fun! Essentially, Ms. Evans soon became more than a family friend, she became family. As time progressed, despite our age differences, she became a very close and trusted confidant of mine, and I feel that I became a daughter to her.

During law school, our relationship really blossomed. Law school was a very challenging time for me. For the first time in my life, I began to battle anxiety and self-doubt. Ms. Evans always called to pray with me and always answered when I called for us to pray together. I called her early in the morning and sometimes late at night. She was always there to offer spiritually based advice. I don't know how she knew, but she always knew when to send a card and exactly what to say in it. Ms. Evans literally prayed me through law school and the Bar Exam. Because of her, I became more confident in my God-given gifts and talents and learned how to exercise in my faith. For that, I am forever grateful to her.

One day I was speaking with Ms. Evans on the telephone, and I told her everyone needs a Lillie. I said this because, Ms. Evans retired from a highly successful career in the Caddo Parish School System. She has single handedly raised two successful children, and she is one of the most spiritually-rooted people I know. All of those things being said, Ms. Evans has the worldly and biblical knowledge and experience that young ladies who are at the beginning of their careers and who are just starting their families need. More importantly, she is not afraid to share her failures and successes so that young women who follow her can have an advantage. One of the most special things about Ms. Evans is that she willingly helps those young women that she feels will benefit from her mentorship, especially when she is directed to do so by the Holy Spirit.

The time I've spent with Ms. Evans over the years will forever remain special to me. Although she is serious about the Word of God, she is not afraid to be human and have fun. Oh my goodness, sometimes me and Ms. Evans just laugh! In the same vein, she has also been here for me during some very dark and uncertain times in my life.

In short, it is hard to describe my relationship with Ms. Evans, because it's so special and unique to us. In summation, "she's my Lillie." It's my sincere prayer that young ladies across the world are blessed and fortunate to find theirs.

JASMINE DOUGLAS

I am fortunate to call Ms. Lillie my mentor, prayer warrior, life coach, friend, and the list goes on and on. When we first met, I did not know that our relationship would flourish to this state. I just knew my mom told me that I would be helping one of her old supervisors who needed help around the house.

Little did I know at the time that I would gain so much in the process. The funny thing is that I cannot recall a date or a time frame when it happened. By that I mean when things shifted from me just cleaning to me gleaning knowledge that would impact my life in such a wonderfully marvelous way.

She became a spiritual mentor, a voice of wisdom, and a voice of clarity. I distinctly recall one conversation we had sitting at her dining room table one Saturday afternoon. I was looking at different colleges and in the process of determining my major. I always wanted to become a physician, but at the time I told her that I wanted to major in nursing. I think it was a combination of fear and anxiety that plagued me, but all I remember was Ms. Evans was "not for it." She looked me square in my face very confused and in so many words told me that I needed to reevaluate that. In retrospect, I just laugh, but Ms. Evans saw that my plan wasn't the plan God had for me and she was one of those messengers who He needed to set me back on track.

Now as a third-year medical student, I can confidently say that seventeen-year-old Jasmine's eyes definitely could not see just how far God would bring twenty-five-year-old Jasmine. It has only been God's grace and people that He has sent in my path like Ms. Evans who has gotten me to this point.

Over the years Ms. Evans has sent cards of encouragement, prayed powerful prayers, given me pamphlets, and so much more to continue to encourage me throughout my life and to let me know that I am not alone. We, as brothers and sisters in Christ must stand, help, and encourage one another. That is one of the most important lessons that I have learned to date with Ms. Evans.

Recently, I took my first Medical School Board Exam. I think that time has to be one of the toughest seasons I have gone through in my life thus far. I am glad to say I made it through, but also that I am spiritually stronger because of it.

I had a conversation with Ms. Evans not too long ago and I told her that I am turning into a "Lillie" and she laughed. By that I mean I wrote cards of encouragements to my classmates and gifted them with the same book that was given to me by Ms. Evans. I understand now there is a ministry in sharing the word of God as there is in receiving. It has brought me closer to some of my classmates and I am all the better for it. I thank God that I have a Lillie in my life. I also will continue to strive be a "Lillie" to others.

ANASTASIA DOUGLAS

My name is Anastasia Douglas. When I was little, I spent a lot of time around my sisters. What I realized is that they spent some time with this woman named Ms. Lillie Evans. I didn't know at the time that Ms. Evans was their mentor. They spent quite some time with her, and then she decided that maybe we should spend some time together too. I was in sixth grade at the time. My life was not in the best shape or form at the time. I started going every other Saturday. I actually enjoyed going for several reasons. One it got me away from doing some chores at home and also I had someone to talk to about my experiences. I had many different things running through my mind during middle school. I always confused right from wrong, but fortunately Ms. Evans was there to help me.

Over time, my mom started to see a change in my attitude and how I acted. Before I went to Ms. Evans, my attitude was horrible; I was never happy about anything. Now I was finally starting to feel happy about life and school. It just takes one person to listen to how you feel to make you feel better. My own personality was found because of Ms. Evans. During middle school, I really didn't have good friends. I thought they were my friends but it turned out they were only my associates. After a while I hung out with other people who were really sweet. Today, I'm still friends with them, and they embrace me as their moral compass.

Going to Ms. Evans' house made me realize who I was. My mom was happier around me and so was my dad. I got up in the morning actually wanting to start my day instead of complaining. It wasn't just my attitude that got better but my life skills as well. I learned how to pray better than I did before. I even learned how to clean up around the house better too. Only the small things in life truly make a difference. I loved going to the store with Ms. Evans because it felt like I was important. We would go sometimes just to get some groceries and we always had a good time. You see everyone needs that special person in their life to help them. It doesn't matter what you are going through, there is always someone to help out. I'm especially happy to have Ms. Evans in my life. Without her influence, I don't know how my life would be right now.

CHAPTER 7

FRIENDS TAKE THEIR EXPERIENCES WITH YOU TO DIFFERENT LEVELS

We may never know how our words, actions, and ideals affect others or when or how it is mind-boggling to discover that what you considered to be an everyday act of kindness profoundly touched someone's life and heart. I have mentored a few young adults, much younger than me, who were experiencing life's hurts of some kind. It has been awesome to see how with prayer and communication, they have succeeded and maintain contact although hundreds of miles away. In other words, we seldom realize the impact of our words, actions, and deeds.

CHERIE COOK

Lillie's Legacy

Serve one another. (Galatians 5:13)

Based on a sermon series message by Shawn Bernard.

Lillie, I am forever grateful for your embodiment of James 5:16, for which Shawn Bernard refers to as, "struggling on behalf of someone else." Selecting your day of every week as Thursday to intercede, so that I may, "stand spiritually mature; fully assured in all of the ways and the will of God for my life." On my death bed, I shall say, "Todah Lillie," for your struggling on behalf of me and my loved ones in prayer as Jesus prays for us (John 17:9).

Just as Robert Murray McShane (1836–1873) said from the Church of Scotland's St. Peter's Church, "If I could hear Christ praying for me in the next room, I would not fear a million enemies. Yet distance makes no difference. He is praying for me."

On most Thursdays, Lillie you embody Romans 8:27. I am resting in truth, "you are most helpful in that which feels helpless" (Shawn Bernard).

James 5:13

The following is the text translations of "thank you" from "Giving Thanks" for an a cappella choir, written in 2016 by Phillip Schroeder

Merci: 1 Thessalonians 5:25 Pray for us

Murakose: Colossians 4:2, 3 Steadfast

Xie' xie: Colossians 4:12 Prayer

Dahkujem: 1 Timothy 3:1 Pray for us

Arigato: Hebrews 13:8 Pray for us

Efharisto: John 17:9 High Priestly prayer

Shunkran: Hebrews 7: 25 Jesus is interceding

Shukyria: James 5:8 Pray for enemies

Spasibo: Hebrews 13:4

Grazie: Romans 8: 3, 4

Gracias:1 Samuel 12:23 Act of Obedience

Pilamayaye: James 5:16 Sanctification

Danke: Ephesians 1: 17

Danku: Ephesians 1:18

Takk, tack: Ephesians 1:19 Immeasurable Grace

Todah 1: Daniel 12:23

Obrigada: Proverbs 3:5–6

Terima kashihb: Jeremiah 29:11

Thank you Romans 5:6

Special Tribute to My Mentor:

Mrs. Rebecca P. Walker

Dear Mrs. Walker,

Words escape me as I attempt to pen words of gratitude to you for accepting me and loving me as a part of your family. Thank you very, very much. Somehow, I don't think it's a coincidence that you, Mrs. Walker, gave so much of your money, talents, and time to help me succeed and years later I received Ashley, your granddaughter into my life to love and help succeed.

Although, our circumstances were different, I always cherished the times I spent with Ashley and her mom, Gail, in honor of your memory. It was just great to have someone from Natchitoches, LA, our hometown seventy miles South of Shreveport, LA.

It was good to have someone with the same upbringing as me. I could relate to their work ethics and saw so many of your characteristics and traits in both of them. Therefore, you were a constant in my memory. I smile as I envision you both in heaven sharing your lists of accomplishments here on earth. In case you are keeping score, you both scored points for sharing your love with me and for that I am most grateful. I am proud to share your worth with the world.

Lillie White

In Honor Of
Rebecca Beatrice Phanor Walker
July 31, 1926 – December 15, 2000

Saturday, December 23, 2000
Viewing: 9:30 a.m. – 10:45 a.m.
Memorial Service: 11:00 a.m.
Burial: Immediately After Service
At St. Martha Baptist Church

First Baptist Church
1116 Amulet Street
Natchitoches, Louisiana

Dr. Joseph D. Dupree, Pastor

OBITUARY

Rebecca Beatrice Phanor Walker, affectionately known as "Beck", "MoDear", "MaMoo", and Sister Walker, was born on July 31, 1926 to Eva Lee Duncantel Phanor and Nathaniel Phanor. She lived in Natchitoches Parish her entire life. She joined the St. Martha Baptist Church at a young age and worked diligently in the church.

Following high school graduation, she became a teacher at St. Augustine. She received the B.S. and M.S. degrees from Grambling State College (now University) in 1953 and 1976, respectively.

During her college life, she met and married Henry Walker. To this union four children were born, Henri Frances (Frankie), L. Diane, J. Gail, and Gregory Mose. Rebecca was dedicated to her family. She provided constant love, support, and Christian example.

Rebecca served as founder, president, secretary, and just a member of many Christian organizations. She worked endlessly to lift up the name of Jesus. Her favorite times were spent going to and working in conventions, associations, meetings, or wherever she felt she could be a steward for the Lord.

Rebecca leaves to cherish her memory: a loving and devoted husband of 51 years, four children, nine grandchildren, three great-grandchildren, two local nieces and a nephew, other nieces and nephews, and a host of cousins, friends, and colleagues.

Special Tribute to the Granddaughter of My Mentor:

Jennifer Ashley Mitchell Carter

I was involved in Ashley's life from a very early age. She became like family to me in much the same way I had been received by my mentor all those years earlier. I believe God sent her to me and my children on occasions when I was struggling as a single parent. Even as a small child, she had great wisdom and was a lot of fun. I took her with me and treated her as one of my children.

Because she was much younger than my two children, I always tried to get her prepared for bed early and involved my children for prayers, stories, etc. before bed. Ashley would always try to drag those times and activities out to stay up longer. She would have us sing, "Jesus Loves Me," several times or ask questions about the stories. Our favorite Ashley story is the time we sung, "Jesus loves me this I know for the Bible tells me so. Yes, Jesus loves me, yes Jesus loves me for the Bible tells me so." "Mama," she asked, "Who is Meso?" My children laughed and I laughed and she joined in the laughter. Of course she got to stay up later as I explained "ME" in the song was all of us, including Ashley.

I got to participate in Ashley's life from toddlerhood through high school and we kept in touch through college, graduate school, and afterward. Her accomplishments speak for themselves.

Jennifer Ashley Mitchell-Carter graduated with honors from the Southern University Nelson Mandela School of Public Policy where she earned a Master of Arts degree in Political Science, while simultaneously earning her Juris Doctorate from the Southern University Law Center in 2011.

As an SULC student, she was elected vice president and president of the National Black Law Students Association, as well as sub-regional director. Additionally, Mrs. Mitchell-Carter served as the Vice President of Entertainment for the Sports and Entertainment Legal Association, a graduate advisor, teaching assistant, and certified mediator in the Southern University Law Center Medication Clinic. Additionally, she worked with the Committee on Small Business and Entrepreneurship, the Senate Personal Office of US Senator Mary Landrieu, and worked as a law clerk for the Department of Business and Legal Affairs for Black Entertainment Television (BET/Viacom) in Washington, D.C. Mrs. Mitchell-Carter held positions with Senate President Pro Tempore Sharon Weston Broome, US District Court, Middle District of Louisiana under Judge James J. Brady, the Louisiana State Senate in the Office of the Chief of Staff, and the Assistant Chief of Staff, Johnny G. Anderson, in the Office of Governor Kathleen Blanco.

Mrs. Mitchell-Carter became the youngest Executive Director of the Louisiana Legislative Black Caucus and the Executive Director of the Louisiana Legislative Black Caucus Foundation. In 2013, she formed Pearson and Mitchell attorneys and Counselors at Law with her partner Robert A. Pearson. Mrs. Mitchell-Carter continued her career as a legislative analyst for the Senate Select Committee on Women and Children and Staff Attorney for the Senate and Governmental Affairs Committee, chaired by Senator Karen Carter Peterson.

Mrs. Mitchell-Carter last served as Director of Governmental Affairs for the University of Louisiana System and adjunct professor of Advanced Legal Writing at the Southern University Law Center.

A native of Shreveport, Louisiana, Mrs. Mitchell-Carter graduated Caddo Parish Magnet High School in 2003 and Louisiana State University and A&M College, where she earned her Bachelor of Arts in Political Science in 2007.

Mrs. Mitchell-Carter was a member of the American Bar Association, Louisiana State Bar Association, Baton Rouge Bar Association, and Louis A. Martinet Legal Society. She was involved in various organizations such as the Delta Sigma Theta Sorority, Inc., where she served as the State Social Action Chair, Walker's Legacy, The Order of the Eastern Star Prince Hall Affiliate, Junior League of Baton Rouge, and Baton Rouge Area Chamber Leadership Program. As a member of New Gideon Baptist Church, she served as the Director of the Jubilant Praise Young Adult Dance and Business Owner Ministries, and actively participated in Vacation Bible School, as well as the Women's and Couples Ministries.

Mrs. Mitchell-Carter and her unborn son were called to their heavenly home on Monday, May 27, 2019, and is survived by her devoted husband, Charles R. Carter, Jr., adoring mother, J. Gail Walker-Mitchell, and host of family, friends, and classmates.

Jennifer Ashley Mitchell-Carter lived her purpose as a faithful and loving servant of God with a passion for positively influencing the lives of others, in particular, young women entering their professional careers.

Jennifer Ashley Mitchell-Carter, Esq.

SHREVEPORT - Jennifer Ashley Mitchell-Carter, Esq. was born on April 16, 1985, in Shreveport, Louisiana. On Monday, May 27, 2019, she and Baby Carter were welcomed home by their Lord and Savior, Jesus Christ. A celebration of life will be held, Friday, June 7, 2019 at 5:30 p.m. at the New Gideon Baptist Church, 2552 Balis Dr., Baton Rouge, Louisiana and will continue on Saturday, June 8, 2019, at 10:00 AM at the Greater King David Baptist Church, 222 Blount Rd., Baton Rouge, Louisiana.

Ashley's memories will be cherished by those left behind; her husband, Charles Ray Carter, Jr.; mother, Jennifer Gail Walker Mitchell; father, James Bennett Mitchell; grandparents, John and Addie Bennett Mitchell, Henry Walker, James Bennett, Sr. and a special grandmother, Rosie J. Jones; father and mother-in-law, Charles Ray, Sr. and Betty Wright Carter; Siblings, JaKeva Mitchell, Julius Mitchell, and Karl Bennett Raggiol; sister and brother-in-law Danielle Carter and Darius Carter, Sr. ; and a host of uncles, aunts, nieces, nephews other relatives, and friends.

In lieu of flowers, memorial contributions may be made to the J. Ashley Mitchell-Carter Scholarship Fund at jamcscholarship.com.

Tips for the Mentors

This book is the result of a mentee expressing sincerely, "Ms. Evans, every child needs a lily." It contains testimonies of services of a mentor and some of the people whose lives she touched, and the story of the people who influenced her work.

The book portrays the importance of care and encouragement from others in addition to family members, and how they can positively impact a child or young adult's life. Just like the Giving Tree, care and encouragement continue to motivate children to do great things in this world because someone chose to care and encourage children.

It is my sincere desire that this book inspires children and youth to share their lives with others to foster love and care to combat violence and other social ills plaguing our society. There is not a "set in stone" way of guiding a life for good growth but prayer, communication, and good listening skills. The activities may vary with each individual, but individual attention is key. The following "Tips for the Mentor" may prove helpful.

1. Decide on the age group, or the child, or person you would like to help.
2. Learn as much as possible about characteristics of the child (a talk with a teacher or parent might suffice).
3. Always provide a "get-acquainted" activity, a short Word of Wisdom, learning activity, Bible scripture to live by or fun activity at each session.
4. Be sure to communicate the goals of the meetings: to assist in any way to help the child become successful and serve as a resource to help them solve whatever problems they are facing.

5. Decide on a meeting place and time that will provide consistent and convenient opportunities for individual attention for at least fifteen minutes for young children and thirty to forty-five minutes of instruction and dialogue followed by a Bible verse discussion and then a fun activity.

<u>Note</u>: The nature of the need for help or the activity chosen for sharing dictate an output of time spent. I always tried to keep activities to thirty minutes with breaks as needed. Visits ranged from two to four hours every other Saturday.

<u>Note</u>: Try to schedule visits to eliminate strangers to the mentees and avoid interactions with strangers. Any activity that involves interaction with adults or other children should be shared with the mentee and parents before meeting.

CONTRIBUTIONS

Many thanks for the unselfish contributions of personal information to make this project possible! It is my sincere hope that this publication will serve as a vehicle much like The Underground Railroad where people will once again trust God to reach out and dare to help others who are trying to become successful. We must take it upon ourselves to help where many government institutions are failing our children. While the schools no longer allow prayer, we must continue to have it in our homes while we can. Care, concern, and listening can inspire people to always do their best. Just a little guidance can produce greatness from many. This project was both rewarding and challenging. The heartfelt stories will always be remembered. Saying, "thank you" to my former teachers means a lot, and featuring the art work of my grandson, Jason Kelly Vallas, when he was but seven years old is awesome. Putting it all together with the help of Joscelin Douglas, my "godsend," can only be described as another divine appointment. Thanks, everybody!

Contributors:

ANASTASIA DOUGLAS

Anastasia L. Douglas is a native of Shreveport, Louisiana. She successfully completed elementary school at Eden Gardens Magnet, and middle school at Caddo Middle Magnet School. While in middle school she wrote a book entitled, How to Survive Middle School, She was inducted into the National Junior Honor Society, and maintained a GPA of 3.7. She is currently a freshman at Caddo Magnet High School in Shreveport, LA. Her future goal and dream is to become a meteorologist.

KARI JOHNSON HARPER

Kari (Johnson) Harper grew up in Shreveport and Lafayette, Louisiana. She graduated from C.E. Byrd High School in Shreveport, and finished her college education at UL-Lafayette with a degree in General Studies. She has worked in banking, education, oil business, criminal court system, law enforcement, and insurance. Currently, she lives in Edmond, Oklahoma, with her husband, Michael, and their daughter, Sidney. Kari works part-time for Wings—a Special Needs community. Wings is a non-profit that works with adults with special needs. She is a member of Edmond Women's Club where she spends her time volunteering with other non-profits in the Edmond community, and is active with her daughter's school's PTO. The Harpers are actively involved in their church, East Edmond Community Church. Kari enjoys spending time with her family, food, interior decorating, reading, and traveling.

CHERIE COOK

I met Lillie in 1995 while we both were engaging as participants in a religion-based therapeutic group, Healing Life's Hurts, led by Anglican Priest, Reverend James Young. During this time, I was hiding behind my fear-filled secret of experiencing an unwanted abortion in 1977. With Lillie becoming my powerful mentoring friend, after meeting in 1995, I began my spiritual journey: leaving my abusive marriage in 1996, and deciding to end my twelve and a half years of abusive relationship with my spouse in 1998; moving from Shreveport, Louisiana, to Mt. Ida, Arkansas, in 1997; pursuing completion of my graduate studies in community counseling, completed in May of 1999 at Henderson State University; becoming a Licensed Associate Counselor to becoming terminally licensed as a Licensed Professional Counselor under the Arkansas Board of Examiners in Counseling in December of 2003. Currently, I am working in Hot Springs, Arkansas, as a DHS-Approved Infant Mental Health Therapist working with populations between the ages of zero to forty-eight months in Child Parent Psychotherapy.

SHERRON PHAE WILLIAMS

Sherron Phae Williams serves as an Assistant City Attorney and Prosecutor for the City of Shreveport. In this position, she serves as an attorney adviser to several city departments, engages in civil litigation, and prosecutes misdemeanors. Additionally, Sherron is the owner of The SPD Firm, LLC. Her firm practice areas consist of business consulting, estate planning, and personal injury. Most recently, Sherron accepted an invitation to work as a writing fellow for the Southern University Law Center. In this position, Sherron assists graduates with preparation for the Louisiana State Bar Examination by serving as a tutor and mentor.

In the community, Sherron serves as co-chair of legislative affairs for NWLA SHRM, a board member for Goodwill Industries of North Louisiana, member and former Law Week co-chair for the Shreveport Bar Association's Young Lawyer Section, and outreach team leader of the Booth-Politz Inn of Court. As a community leader and public servant, Sherron is often called on to speak at community events to motivate youth. Sherron is an active member of the New Bethel Baptist Church.

Sherron received her B.S. from Southern University A&M College, where she graduated magna cum laude, and her law degree from Southern University Law Center. She is married to Maurice Williams and they have one daughter, Adara Aeryn.

STEPHANIE COSME

Stephanie Cosme, pastoral assistant for The Oaks of Louisiana, has been in caregiving for more than twenty-five years. She began her career in the healthcare field as a certified nursing assistant in 1994. She has worked in many areas of direct patient care including post-operative, geriatric psychiatry, hospice, emergency, and cardiac step down. She has an associate degree in general science from Bossier Parish Community College and an associate degree in general studies from Northwestern State University. "I still take care of people, just in a different way," she says. As pastoral assistant, Cosme has an integral role in spiritual life programs and practices at The Oaks including Communion, bedside prayer, Bible studies, and end-of-life celebration for residents, among others.

She also directs The Oaks of Louisiana Chorus. Cosme, a native of Smackover, AK, has lived in Shreveport, LA, since 1974. She is a lifelong member of the Assembly of God church and attends Gateway Church where she is involved in food pantry, compassion ministries, and music. Cosme considers it an honor and a privilege to serve residents of The Oaks of Louisiana. In addition to her role at The Oaks of Louisiana, Cosme also is pastoral assistant for Willis-Knighton Health System.

Joyce Carter

Lillie and Joyce's friendship, which spans for more than thirty years, began when they met while working in the Caddo Parish School System. Joyce Carter is a retired elementary school educator, a master teacher with over forty years of contribution and cultivating student-focus settings to achieve maximum learning experiences.

Throughout her career Joyce only had—and still has—one goal and that is to motivate every kid she encounters to reach his/her full potential. She has received numerous awards, honors, and recognitions throughout her career. Her professional affiliations include Phi Delta Kappa Fraternity, and she is a life member of the National Education Association. Joyce is also active in her community through her church and through her sorority, Alpha Kappa Alpha Sorority, Incorporated.

JASMINE DOUGLAS

Jasmine Dominique Douglas is currently a third-year medical student at Saint Louis University School of Medicine. She is involved in multiple organizations such as the Student National Medical Association, where she is currently a Health and Policy Legislative Fellow. This national fellowship focuses on conveying the importance of policy and how it affects direct patient care. She is also a Rodney M. COE program participant. This graduation distinction places an emphasis on community service throughout all four years of medical school. Jasmine is also a published author: *Low High-Density Lipoprotein and Psychopathology: A Review in the Annals of Clinical Psychiatry and Why Every Student Should Go to Rehab in Grand Rounds*, SLU alumni magazine.

In the community, Jasmine currently serves as the Health Ministry Leader at the Cathedral at Pleasant Grove in St. Louis, MO. She has implemented health programs where members have lost collectively over a hundred pounds. She also hosts educational sessions on common healthcare issues giving members of the community an opportunity to ask questions about their health. She is passionate about patient advocacy and health literacy.

Jasmine received her B.S. in biology with a minor in chemistry from Xavier University of Louisiana, where she graduated magna cum laude. Upon graduation from Saint Louis University School of Medicine, Jasmine plans to pursue a career in Family Medicine with an emphasis on the urban population.

DJENIELE HOOTEN

Dejeniele Hooten was born and raised for half of her life in the Pacific Northwest in Yakima, Washington. She is the oldest of five children: Dejeniele, Dominique, Dewitt, Judah, and Mya, all Jones. When she was around the age of sixteen, she and her entire family uprooted their lives in Yakima, Washington, and traded it in for a new and interesting one in the South. Dejeniele Jones Hooten would attend Evangel Christian Academy where she would graduate in 2005. After graduation she would become a member of the touring family band *Forever Jones*. The group would go on to be nominated for five Stellar Awards and would win one of them. They were also nominated for the Dove Award and Grammy in 2010. During her time at SCC she would meet her husband, Nathaniel Hooten, and they would both serve for about fifteen years under the leadership of Pastors Denny and Deanza Duron.

Soon God would guide them to Life Church, where she and her husband would be worship pastors for a little over a year under the loving leadership of Pastors Gary and Shelia Cavalier. They would come to a point where they would feel the Lord calling them once again and they would soon find themselves at Gateway Church, where she and her husband would serve under the wonderful leadership of Pastors Dusty and Chantal Small.

Dejeniele is a mother of three beautiful children: Madison, twelve, Mackenzie, eight, and Maxamillion, three; all three are very musical and incredibly active and loving. Dejeniele Jones Hooten resides in Shreveport, LA, where she would commute to Dallas, Texas, to help her family's ministry, *Forever Jones*, under the leadership of Dewitt and Kim Jones.

ANGELA DOUGLAS

Angela L. Douglas is married to Melvin R. Douglas and together they have three beautiful children: Sherron, Jasmine, and Anastasia.

Mrs. Douglas is a retired educator with thirty plus years of experience in education. She began her career as a fourth grade teacher and taught fourth grade in a neighborhood school and a magnet school for twelve combined years. Mrs. Douglas soon rose through the ranks of administration first as a curriculum coordinator, then instructional coordinator, assistant principal, and finally principal of Forest Hill Elementary School, the same school where she began her teaching career.

In the community, Mrs. Douglas works in various capacities in her church, including adult women's Sunday School teacher, co-sponsor of the Youth Department, co-director of Vacation Bible School, member of the Deaconess Board, and the Scholarship Committee. She also participates in Bible Study Fellowship (BSF), enjoying learning more about the Word of God.

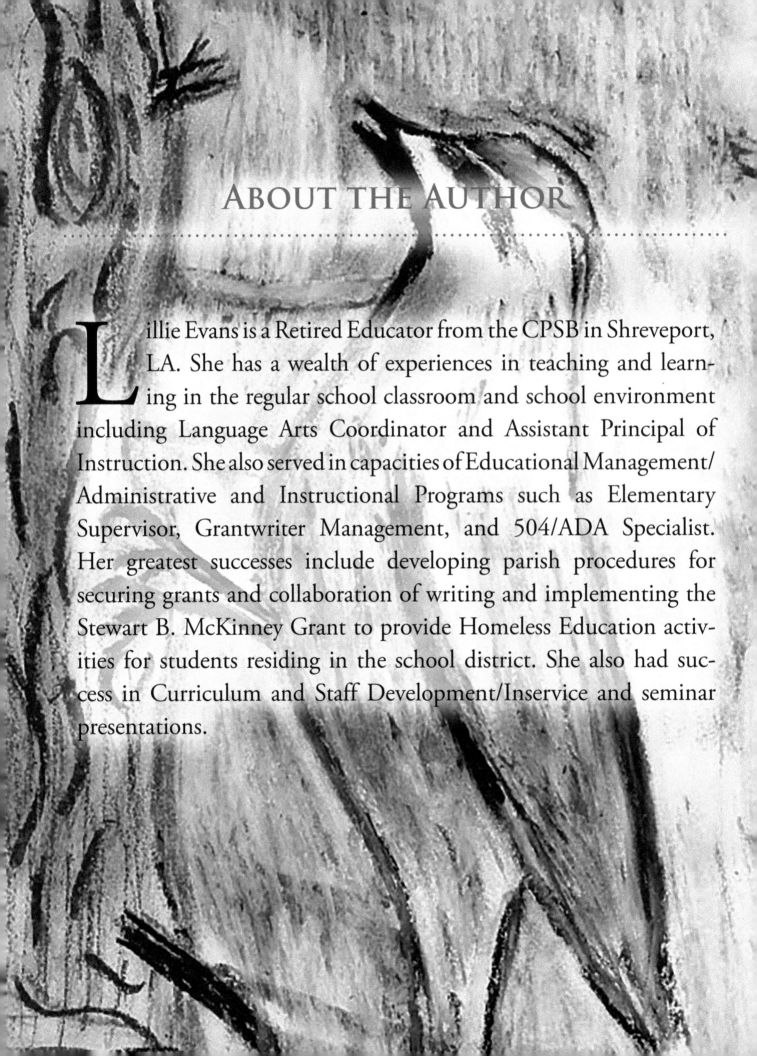

ABOUT THE AUTHOR

Lillie Evans is a Retired Educator from the CPSB in Shreveport, LA. She has a wealth of experiences in teaching and learning in the regular school classroom and school environment including Language Arts Coordinator and Assistant Principal of Instruction. She also served in capacities of Educational Management/Administrative and Instructional Programs such as Elementary Supervisor, Grantwriter Management, and 504/ADA Specialist. Her greatest successes include developing parish procedures for securing grants and collaboration of writing and implementing the Stewart B. McKinney Grant to provide Homeless Education activities for students residing in the school district. She also had success in Curriculum and Staff Development/Inservice and seminar presentations.